DEDICATION

In memory of all those who have fought and
given their lives to establish and maintain the
United States of America as one nation under God.

In honor of all those who continue to fight today.

A CHRISTIAN'S GUIDE TO
PRAYING SCRIPTURES THAT WORK
FOR THE 21ST CENTURY

Pray

AMERICA
GREAT AGAIN

RUTH ANN NYLEN

PRAY AMERICA GREAT AGAIN: A Christian's Guide to Praying Scriptures
That Work for the 21st Century
Copyright © 2025 Ruth Ann Nylen
Books published by Mobilize Press are available at special discounts for bulk
purchases in the United States of America by ministries and other
organizations. For more information, please contact the publisher.
Mobilize Press, P.O. Box 36, Land O' Lakes, FL 34639, or e-mail to:
inquiry@mobilizepress.com

Library of Congress Control Number: 2025921197

Title: PRAY AMERICA GREAT AGAIN: A Christian's Guide to Praying
Scriptures That Work for the 21st Century

ISBN: 978-0-9839130-4-7

Cover and interior design: Anna Hoffman
Printed in the United States of America

ALSO BY RUTH ANN NYLEN

The Radical Power of God

My Sermon Journal

Scan for more
resources and
to connect with
the author.

PURPOSE OF THIS GUIDE

This guide is intended to inspire, equip, and mobilize Christian believers to pray for America.

The greatest weapon in the fight to maintain the United States of America is the prayed and declared word of God, in faith, by a believer in Jesus Christ.

Praying and applying scripture to any and every situation is without limit, because the word of God is limitless.

Prayer is not a stagnant entity. Rather, it is a fluid, ever-evolving communication with God that is best led by His Spirit. God's word is alive because Jesus is alive. We are to be led by the Spirit of God, praying the word, as life and circumstances unfold.

I invite you to pray for America with me.

Ruth Ann

Are you a Christian believer? Scan for more.

Table Of Contents

Introduction

THOUGHTS ON PRAYER FOR AMERICA

➤ All things have been created by Jesus and are sustained by His word. (John 1:3; Hebrews 1:3)

➤ The Bible is the word of God. Believers are commanded to take up the sword of the Spirit, which is the word of God. (Ephesians 6:17)

➤ The spoken word of God in prayer wields the sword of the Spirit as a weapon. Unless used with intention and skill, a weapon has no effect.

➤ Declaring the word of God is the most powerful force for change on earth. It can change anything because it penetrates the human heart as nothing else can. (Hebrews 4:12)

➤ Prayer activates the power of God's Spirit to bring change. All change comes 'Not by might nor by power, but by my Spirit,' says the Lord Almighty. (Zechariah 4:6)

➤ America needs change and restoration to God.

➤ Prayer is the pathway to the change.

WHY PRAY?

Consider these two Biblical reasons to pray:

First, God commands us to pray.

> *Rejoice always, pray continually, give thanks in all circumstances; for this is God's will for you in Christ Jesus. (1 Thessalonians 5:16-18)*

Second, prayer puts skin on our faith. If we want something to change, we need to do something.

> *"But someone will say, 'you have faith; I have deeds.'" Show me your faith without deeds, and I will show you my faith by my deeds. (James 2:18)*

The United States of America is great because it was established under God. American currency and the Pledge of Allegiance both declare the United States of America is "one nation under God." Because America belongs to God, its return to greatness must go both to and through God. How does America go through God? America goes through God when people pray.

WHAT NEEDS TO CHANGE?

Most of us probably don't need to look too far to see things that are not right. Decisions and actions aligned with God's word were once societal norms in America. Today, some of God's foundational truths have become twisted or left to personal interpretation. God is no longer most important to many Americans. Too many have elected to make God optional.

People

are not the

problem.

SECTORS OF SOCIETY

Sectors of American society have begun to fracture. Destructive and eroding forces have damaged and harmed many people. If left unchecked, irreversible damage may result. At least three writers, including Johnny Enlow, Bill Bright and Loren Cunningham, have identified seven sectors that influence societies. These sectors are the government, the economy (also sometimes described as commerce, science, and technology), religion, education, family, arts and entertainment, and media. (Read more about the seven sectors, also called mountains, and their scriptural basis in the references at the end of this book.)

FIVE ELEMENTS OF EFFECTIVE PRAYER

01 **PRAY ON TARGET.**

God calls things aligned with His word righteous. Anything not aligned with God's word, He calls unrighteous. Prayer aimed at maintaining or restoring righteous alignment with God's word is effective.

The problems plaguing every sector of American society are instigated by underlying, unrighteous, and wicked spiritual forces that cause people to act in ways that harm others and are not aligned with God's will for mankind. **People are not the problem.** Therefore, we don't pray against people. We pray against evil forces, as Paul said:

> *For our struggle is not against flesh and blood, but against the rulers, against the authorities, against the powers of this dark world, and against the spiritual forces of evil in the heavenly realms. (Ephesians 6:12)*

The **only** spiritual weapon is prayer. Effective change only comes when the full power of God's word is unleashed on the underlying

6

spiritual force. It is essential to understand and embrace that the root cause of unrighteous actions is not the people carrying out the action. This is why arguing and fighting with people never works. Rather, we attack the underlying force behind the behavior. Otherwise, the problem may be suppressed for a season, but it will never be completely removed. Because the underlying cause is spiritual, the fight must occur in the spirit realm. Prayer and declaration of God's word is the only solution, because the battle is spiritual. Each of the seven sectors of American society needs and can benefit from faith-filled prayer.

02 PRAY FOR RIGHTEOUSNESS IN AMERICA.

Praying for righteousness means we pray for God's plan and purpose for everything on earth to operate in alignment with His word. This confirms we are praying as Jesus replied to His disciples, when asked how to pray:

"This, then, is how you should pray: 'Our Father in heaven, hallowed be your name, your kingdom come, your will be done, on earth as it is in heaven…' (Matthew 6:9-10)

Praying in accordance with the word of God invites the Kingdom of God to come to earth. God's word is always aligned with God's will, plan and purpose.

03 PRAY AGAINST UNRIGHTEOUSNESS IN AMERICA.

Praying against unrighteousness means we pray against the spiritual forces seeking to establish things not aligned with God's word. When the underlying spiritual force is put under the word of God in prayer, people's actions that are not aligned with God's word will change.

04 PRAY AND DECLARE GOD'S WORD.

Despite all that can go wrong, God has not left believers without a remedy to combat unrighteousness on earth. God has established the declaration of His word in prayer as the method to activate His power over everything on earth. God's will is God's word. Therefore, praying the word of God over America will re-establish His will. There are two reasons why Christians must pray God's word. First, God tells us to remind Him of His promises.

Isaiah 43:26 says:

> *"Review the past for me, let us argue the matter together; state the case for your innocence."*

When we remind God of the promises in His word, it reminds us and establishes our faith in God to perform His word. As believers confess His promises and bring them before His throne of grace, He responds. Jesus said we will receive what we ask for when we pray His word.

> *If you remain in me and my words remain in you, ask whatever you wish, and it will be done for you. (John 15:7)*

The key is that our hearts and minds remain in the word of God and the word of God remains in us. Increasing our familiarity with God's word enables us to bring it back to the Lord in prayer and remind Him of His promises.

Second, praying God's word is God's plan. The most effective and powerful method to change and realign societal wrongs or imbalances is to pray and declare the word of God. When a Christian combines his or her faith with speaking the living word of God, God begins to move. God said His word never returns to Him void or is

The most effective and powerful method to change and realign societal wrongs or imbalances is to pray and declare the word of God.

without effect. It will always accomplish the purpose for which He sent it. Written about 700 years before Christ, the prophet Isaiah declared this truth:

"As the heavens are higher than the earth, so are my ways higher than your ways and my thoughts than your thoughts. As the rain and the snow come down from heaven, and do not return to it without watering the earth and making it bud and flourish, so that it yields seed for the sower and bread for the eater, so is my word that goes out from my mouth: It will not return to me empty, but will accomplish what I desire and achieve the purpose for which I sent it..." (Isaiah 55: 9-11)

In summary, God has established the declaration of His word in prayer to activate His power over every unrighteous thing on earth. For the nation living under God, prayer holds the power to mend societal fractures. Praying scripture activates a move of God.

05 PRAY WITH SPIRITUAL AUTHORITY.

Believers in Jesus Christ have authority because Jesus gave it to us. Jesus gave His disciples authority as recorded in both Matthew and Luke.

Jesus called His twelve disciples to him and gave them authority to drive out impure spirits and to heal every disease and sickness. (Matthew 10:1)

When Jesus had called the Twelve together, he gave them power and authority to drive out all demons and to cure diseases, and he sent them out to proclaim the kingdom of God and to heal the sick. (Luke 9:1)

Christians have full authority over wicked spiritual forces. Jesus defeated the works of the devil when He rose from the dead. Concurrent with the finished work of Jesus through His resurrection from the dead is the truth that every born-again Christian has received the power and authority to interrupt and destroy ungodly works of the enemy. The destruction of these forces will be fully manifested only after Christians take their authority and use it boldly. Jesus said we will do these works:

> *Very truly I tell you, whoever believes in me will do the works I have been doing, and they will do even greater things than these because I am going to the Father. And I will do whatever you ask in my name, so that the Father may be glorified in the Son. You may ask me for anything in my name, and I will do it. (John 14:12-14)*

HOW TO USE THESE PRAYERS

This book contains a prayer for America and one for each sector of society. These prayers serve as a foundation for praying for America. They may also serve as a starting point for expanded prayer. Each prayer is followed by suggestions to help you develop more prayer specific to your own location, interests, and concerns. Be encouraged to expand and develop prayers with a prayer team, small group, church, or community network, as the Spirit leads.

GUIDE TO PREPARING EXPANDED PRAYERS

Reminders

- Pray for people, by name if you can obtain them, and their families.

- Pray for righteous influence and elimination of unrighteous actions and influence.

- Always pray against unrighteous spiritual forces, not against people.

- Use the included prayers as a guide.

11

Keys to Praying in Faith

Before you begin, decide what you are going to ask God for, based on His word. Include these elements in your prayers:

- Remind God what He said about the prayers you ask in faith in Jesus' Name. (John 16:23)

- Remind God what He said about the necessity of your faith in Him. (Hebrews 11:6)

- Find the specific promise(s) in the word on which you are standing in faith. Then declare these promises. Ask God to perform His word in the life or situation you are praying about.

- Tell God that you receive what He says in His word, now, by faith. (Hebrews 11:1; 2 Corinthians 5:7; Philippians 4:6)

- Close with "in the name of Jesus, Amen." (John 14:14)

Scan for access to FREE Prayer of Faith Worksheets.

WHO SHOULD PRAY THESE PRAYERS?

- **Individual Believers.** Pray alone in faith. Prayers of a believer based on God's word and offered in faith have great power and please God. (John 16:23; Hebrews 11:6)

- **Two Believers.** Pray in faith and agreement with another believer. Jesus said anything asked by two believers in agreement will be done by God the Father. (Matthew 18:19)

- **Multiple believers.** Pray a prepared prayer in unity with multiple believers. The early church experienced the extreme power of God during united prayer. (Acts 4:23-31)

WHEN TO PRAY

- Pray daily.

- Consider praying for one of the seven sectors on the same day each week.

- Never surrender.

- Pray and declare the word until God brings the change.

- Use this acronym: P.U.S.H. Pray Until Something Happens!

Notes

PRAYER FOR AMERICA

Heavenly Father, your word says the nation whose God is the Lord is blessed. I declare you as Lord over the United States of America. I ask you to pour your blessings on America, according to your word. America was established under your hand and word and therefore is a blessed nation. (Psalm 33:12)

Lord, I declare your memory will be perpetuated through all generations of America and we will praise you for ever and ever. (Psalm 45:17)

Your word says we are a chosen people, a royal priesthood, a holy nation, and your special possession, so we may declare the praises of Jesus Christ who called us out of darkness into your wonderful light. I declare you have established the United States as your treasured possession. (1 Peter 2:9)

According to your word, a nation and people who are obedient to your commands will be blessed coming in and going out. You said we will be blessed in the city and blessed in the country. You said you will set the obedient nation high above all the nations on earth. Lord, you also said that the enemies who rise up against you will be defeated before you. They will come at us from one direction but flee from you in seven. Let America be the nation that is humbled before you and obedient to your word that these promises will be fulfilled. (Deuteronomy 28:1-7)

In our obedience, you will establish us as your holy people, and all the peoples on earth will see that we are called by the name of the Lord. (Deuteronomy 28:10-11)

Lord, you promised to open the heavens from where all blessings flow. You will send rain on our land in season and bless all the work of our hands. We will lend to many nations but will borrow from none. You will make us the head, not the tail, above and not beneath. (Deuteronomy 28:12-13)

I declare and pray the people of America are obedient to you alone. I call and declare a spiritual awakening to you alone. I pray for American hearts to turn to you as Lord.

I pray the sword of the Spirit, which is your spoken word in prayer, will be continually declared over America. (Ephesians 6:17)

I ask all these things, according to your word. On behalf of my nation, the USA, I receive your covenant promises for transformation and abundant blessings of this great nation you have established. In the name of Jesus, I pray. Amen.

Heavenly Father, your word says the nation whose God is the Lord is blessed. I declare you as Lord over the United States of America.

PRAYER FOR GOVERNMENT

All levels of government, local, state, and national

Lord, you have urged us to first pray, bring our petitions, stand in the gap, and give thanks for all those in authority, so that we may live quiet lives in all godliness and holiness. So, Lord, I present to you every government leader in America. I ask for your divine protection, guidance, and wisdom to surround and rule the minds of elected officials and their families. (1 Timothy 2:1-2)

Lord, your word says that all things will be given to those who first seek your kingdom and righteousness. I ask you to establish and order the thoughts of every elected and appointed official in a government position from the local to the presidential. Lord, prompt them, by your Holy Spirit, to seek and hunger for you first and your righteousness. (Matthew 6:33)

According to your word, the heart of a leader or king rests in your hands like a stream to flow wherever you desire. I ask you to take the heart of every government official in your hands. Mold their heart and move them according to your will for America. (Proverbs 21:1)

You have declared that when the righteous rule, the people rejoice and when the wicked rule, the people groan. Therefore, I ask you to fill every leadership position in America with men and women who live righteously and govern according to your word. (Proverbs 29:2)

When speaking of ungodly leaders, Jesus said "Every plant that my heavenly Father has not planted will be pulled up by the roots." Lord, I ask you to pull up and remove every leader not planted by you. (Matthew 15:13) Lord, I pray for every government official to submit to you first so they will govern by your plan and will for America. (James 4:7)

Through the prophet, Micah, you said you require people to act justly, to love mercy, and to walk humbly with you. You promise to bless those who act justly and always do what is right. I pray for government leaders at every level, from local, city, and county officials to our President, to humbly walk with you, to love mercy rather than judgment, and to treat all people fairly and with justice, according to your word. (Psalm 106:3; Micah 6:8)

You have declared in Romans 13:1, that every government authority has been established by you. Therefore, let every government authority have a heart that is molded to do what is right in your sight. I pray for city and county officials, state government officials, and every member of the United States Congress in the House of Representatives, and the Senate.

I pray for the President and Vice President of the United States of America. I pray all leaders and officials in authority act with diligence, integrity, and justice, by making the right decisions for the people they lead and govern. (Romans 12:8) May their actions serve the people in this nation to live peaceful and quiet lives.
(1 Timothy 2:1-2)

Lord, you have said we are not to be overcome by evil, but overcome evil with good. Lord, I ask you to instill the desire in every government worker in America to choose to do good and not respond or react to any evil work with evil. (Romans 12:21)

I pray for the Supreme Court Justices, and all levels of judges for your divine direction, wisdom, and protection. You have said the Holy Spirit will guide us into all truth. Therefore, I ask that you guide them into decisions that are just, right, and align with your truth. (John 16:13)

I ask all these things, according to your word. By faith I receive these spoken covenant promises for the restoration of the American government, in the name of Jesus. *Amen.*

I ask you to take the heart of every government official in your hands.

Mold their heart and move them according to your will for America.

SUGGESTIONS FOR EXPANDED PRAYERS FOR GOVERNMENT

Research and consider expanding your prayers for the following:

- Elected and appointed local, city and county officials

- Local government service personnel. For example, roads and infrastructure, water management, budgets and laws and regulations, libraries, parks and recreation and other services

- US Military locations and personnel, including the Army, Navy, Marines, Air Force, Coast Guard, Space Force and National Guard

- Local public safety including law enforcement, fire and rescue personnel. Pray for their safety, wisdom, divine protection, and mental health. Pray for their families

- Elected and appointed state government representatives and officials. Pray for righteous legislation and policy implementation in your state

Scan for free, step-by-step worksheets to prepare your expanded prayers.

PRAYER FOR EDUCATION

Prayer Focus

All levels of school, pre-K through high school, colleges and universities, vocational and trade training schools

Father, I come to you in the name of Jesus for the education system in the United States of America. I declare your word that says you are the Most High over all the earth and you are exalted above all gods. Therefore, I declare that you are over and above all education in America. (Psalm 97:9)

Lord, you have declared that your Holy Spirit will guide us into all truth. (John 16:13) Today, I seek the mighty hand of your Holy Spirit to hover over and guide every school teacher, administrator, student, and school board member to walk by the Spirit and not gratify the desires of their flesh. (Genesis 1:2; Galatians 5:16) I declare today, according to your word, that every local school teacher is rooted and established in the love of God. (Ephesians 3:17)

According to your word, you give us sound learning and we should not turn against your teaching. I ask you to fill every teacher with sound learning from you so they may impart it to students. (Proverbs 4:2)

Lord, I pray that grace and peace reign in classrooms in abundance through the knowledge of God and our Lord Jesus Christ.
(2 Peter 1:2)

Lord, you have said we are to "start children off on the way they should go, and even when they are old they will not turn from it." I declare every school curriculum in America will teach children what is right. (Proverbs 22:6) I bind the implementation of any unrighteous curriculum in any school system in America today and call it null and void. (Matthew 18:18) Lord, you have called us to have nothing to do with the fruitless deeds of darkness, but rather expose them. You said it is shameful even to mention what the disobedient do in secret. (Ephesians 5:11-12). Therefore, Lord, reveal and expose every wrong or wicked idea that anyone would seek to teach our children.

Today, Lord, I pray school board members would be guided by your truth as you establish their thoughts for decisions promoting goodness and wisdom for the education, protection, and success of every student. (Proverbs 29:2)

Father, your word says to ask you to give us the desires of our hearts and make all our plans succeed. I pray you would give every student the desire of their heart and make all their plans succeed.
(Psalm 20:4)

Lord, you said that good things and joy come to those who seek your wisdom. I ask you to fill every teacher and student with great joy as they explore and learn good things. Let wisdom enter their hearts and knowledge fill their souls with pleasant things.
(Proverbs 2:9-10)

You have said that you have good plans to prosper and give hope and a future to your people. I pray every student in America will learn your ways and that their education will equip them with tools and opportunities to develop and fulfill their God-given purpose. (Jeremiah 29:11)

Lord, you fill us with skills for a good purpose. I pray for intellectual development and increase. I pray for skills and abilities to be developed through sound teaching and learning in our education system. (Exodus 35:30-35)

Lord, you have said it is you who gives us the ability to produce wealth. I pray that college, technical and trade training and education is structured to develop wisdom and critical thinking skills in every student so that they may succeed and prosper in their personal and professional life. (Deuteronomy 8:18; Proverbs 4:7)

Lord, you desire all people to live according to the Spirit of God and not according to their flesh. I declare every school principal in America is led by the Spirit of God, and not controlled by a sinful nature. (Romans 8:5-9) Your word says that what others intend for harm, you intend for our good. (Genesis 50:20) Therefore, Lord, I pray for the exposure and removal of any person in the education system, at any level, seeking to control, manipulate, or otherwise harm any student in any way. (Proverbs 2:22; Matthew 15:13)

According to your word, you will keep us from all harm and watch over our lives. Father, I pray for your divine protection for every student at every level in America. (Psalm 12:7; Psalm 121:7)

I ask all these things according to your word. By faith, I receive these spoken covenant promises for our American education system. Lord, let it flourish and bring America to a brighter future. I thank you for your faithfulness to perform your word. In Jesus' name, I pray, Amen.

Father,
I pray for your
divine protection for
every student at
every level in
America.

SUGGESTIONS FOR EXPANDED PRAYERS
FOR EDUCATION

Research and consider expanding your prayers for the following:

- Teachers, classroom assistants and substitute teachers

- Administrators, principals, and school board members

- Coaches and counselors

- Specific classrooms or programs

- Local school curriculum and its content

- Local technical and trade schools

- Local colleges and universities

Scan for free, step-by-step worksheets to prepare your expanded prayers.

Notes

PRAYER FOR MEDIA AND COMMUNICATION

News entities, television, podcasts, the Internet, social media, advertising

Father, in the name of Jesus, I come to you today with thanksgiving for the American media and communications entities. (Psalm 100:4)

Lord, you alone are God and I declare that you are Lord over all communications in America from this day forward. (Psalm 97:9)

According to your word, those whose ways are blameless, who walk according to the law of the Lord are blessed. Lord, you desire we speak the truth from our heart and avoid any tongue that slanders or casts a slur on others. I pray every person working in a public communications arena would be one whose walk is blameless and who does what is right. I pray you will prompt them to hold their tongue and stop slanderous words from escaping their lips.
(Psalm 15:2-3; Psalm 119:1; Colossians 3:8)

I pray you would silence every flattering lip or boastful tongue, according to your word. (Psalm 12:3)

Lord, you have said that a discerning person keeps wisdom in view but a fool's eyes wander the ends of the earth. Therefore, let everyone who communicates via any form of media exercise discernment and wisdom, not allowing their eyes to be foolish and wander to anything unrighteousness. (Proverbs 17:24)

Lord, you have said we are not to let any unwholesome talk come out of our mouths, but only what helps build others up according to their needs, and that it may benefit those who listen. I pray media personnel intentionally choose to place a guard over their mouth so that no corrupt words or unwholesome talk comes out of it. I pray all communications are used to build others up according to their needs and benefit all those who listen. (Ephesians 4:29)

Lord, I pray that consumers of media in America would choose to feast on gracious words that are sweet to the soul and healing to the bones. (Proverbs 16:24)

Lord, your word says the words of the reckless pierce like swords, but the tongue of the wise brings healing. So, Lord, I bind and block every reckless word before it escapes any lips. Lord, let every media communicator, especially those on television and the Internet, choose and use their words wisely and bring healing to the listener. (Proverbs 12:18)

Lord, you have told us not to look with approval on anything vile and to have no part in what faithless people do. Therefore, Lord, I ask you to give supernaturally discerning eyes and ears to every listener in America. Give people the courage to quickly turn away from anything ungodly. (Psalm 101:3)

Jesus, you said that I have the power and authority to bind up what is wrong. I curse and bind any unrighteous content that seeks to set itself up against the truth and wrongly influence or manipulate Americans. (Matthew 18:18)

By faith, I receive these spoken covenant promises for all American media and communications including news, television, podcasts, the Internet, social media, and advertising. I thank you that you are faithful to perform your word. In Jesus' name, I pray, *Amen.*

Lord, your word says the words of the reckless pierce like swords, but the tongue of the wise brings healing.

So, Lord, I bind and block every reckless word before it escapes any lips.

SUGGESTIONS FOR EXPANDED PRAYERS FOR MEDIA AND COMMUNITCATIONS

Research and consider expanding your prayers for the following:

- Local and national television and radio personnel

- Podcasts and other Internet-based communicators or influencers

- Social media channels

- Advertisers

PRAYER FOR FAMILY

Parents, children, singles, sexual morality

Father, in the name of Jesus I come to you today and declare your word that says everyone in the United States of America has been created in your image as male or female. (Genesis 1:26)

Your word says we are to be devoted to one another in love, honoring one another above ourselves. I pray you would fill the hearts of every family member with devoted love and desire to honor one another above themselves. Lord, bring an end to selfishness. (Romans 12:10)

Lord, you declared John the Baptist would come before Jesus in the spirit and power of Elijah to turn the hearts of parents to their children and to make them ready for you. Lord, I pray for a softened heart of every parent in America so they faithfully turn to their children to lead, guide, and direct them on the right path. (Luke 1:17)

Through the Apostle Paul, you said you are pleased when children obey their parents in everything. I pray children are properly taught and learn to obey their parents in everything to please the Lord. (Colossians 3:20)

Father, your word declares we are to strive for full restoration of relationships, encourage one another, be of one mind, and live in peace. And then, you will be with us. You also said you are close to the brokenhearted and save those who are crushed in spirit. I pray that broken families in America diligently seek reconciliation and restoration. I pray for the presence of the Holy Spirit to comfort and hold the broken-hearted in your arms of love. Father, lift them up and show them your goodness and love. (2 Corinthians 13:11; Psalm 34:18)

Father, your word says "A rod and a reprimand impart wisdom, but a child left undisciplined disgraces its mother." You also said disciplining children will give us peace and bring the delights a parent desires. I pray that parents in the United States would properly discipline their children so that they might live productive, good and godly lives. (Proverbs 29:15, 17)

Lord, you have said that children should not have to save up for their parents, but parents for their children. I pray that parents are financially prudent, choosing to save and provide an inheritance for their children. (2 Corinthians 12:14)

Father, you said that a wife of noble character is worth far more than rubies and her husband has full confidence in her. So, Lord, I pray every man who desires to marry seeks and finds a wife of noble character. Father, give husbands and wives good judgment and let them hear your voice leading them.
(Proverbs 31:10; John 10:27)

According to your word, marriage should be honored by all and the marriage bed kept pure. I pray and declare husbands and wives in America remain faithful to one another for life. (Hebrews 13:4)

Lord, your word instructs us to serve wholeheartedly, as if you were serving the Lord, not people. I declare in the name of Jesus today, that every household in America chooses to serve you, Lord God. (Joshua 24:15; Ephesians 6:7)

In Jesus' name, I declare and receive all these promises for families in America, by faith in your word. Amen.

I pray that broken families in America diligently seek reconciliation and restoration.

I pray for the presence of the Holy Spirit to comfort and hold the broken-hearted in your arms of love.

SUGGESTIONS FOR EXPANDED PRAYERS FOR FAMILY

Research and consider expanding your prayers for the following:

- **Single adults**

- **Marriages**

- **Single parents**

- **Children without parents and foster homes**

- **Runaways**

- **Families experiencing disasters**

- **Adoption**

- **Pregnancy centers**

Scan for free, step-by-step worksheets to prepare your expanded prayers.

PRAYER FOR ARTS AND ENTERTAINMENT

Prayer Focus

Television, movies, social media,
the Internet, graphic and creative arts

Heavenly Father, your word says gracious words are a honeycomb, sweet to the soul and healing to the bones. I come to you today for the arts and entertainment industry in America. I pray and declare that all new movies will be filled with gracious words that bring healing to our nation. (Proverbs 16:24)

Lord, your word warns us to guard our heart, because everything we do flows from it. I pray both producers and consumers of all types of art and entertainment will intentionally guard their hearts, including their eyes and ears. I pray consumers will turn away and refuse to view or consume any kind of art or entertainment that seeks to corrupt the good heart you desire. (Proverbs 4:23)

Lord, you have said we are to give careful thought to the paths for our feet, always looking forward, not turning to the left or right and keeping our feet from evil. I pray for an awakening in the souls of every American. Let all be forewarned to seek goodness and avoid wickedness in any kind of art or entertainment. (Proverbs 4:25-27)

Father, you have said we are to keep our mouths free of perversity and corrupt talk. Therefore, I declare a spiritual guard is placed over the mouths of producers of art and entertainment so that no evil content is produced or distributed. (Proverbs 4:24)

Speaking through the Apostle Paul, you said the veil is taken away when anyone turns to you. I pray and declare that the veil of deception is removed from all those who are producing art and entertainment. Reveal yourself to any who do not know you. Bring them to repentance to choose you as both Savior and Lord. I ask you to raise godly writers, producers, and actors who boldly move forward to prepare righteous and wholesome content, suitable for viewing by all Americans. (2 Corinthians 3:16)

Father, I ask that you fill the heart and mind of every artist and creator with good things and not evil, for Lord, you have said that the mouth speaks what the heart is full of. (Luke 6:45)

Lord Jesus, you said whatever I bind on earth will be bound in heaven, and whatever I loose on earth will be loosed in heaven. I now bind and curse the celebration and glorification of death, destruction, and evil in movies and video games. Lord, I loose and call for video game developers to create games that challenge and build analytical thinking skills that establish tools for effective life and business skills. (Matthew 18:18; Mark 11:21)

Father, your word tells us to ask you if we need wisdom for anything and you will freely give it to us without finding us at fault. I pray your Spirit will prompt and fill everyone in America with a desire to seek your wisdom so they can rightly discern art and entertainment that is pure and worthy of viewing. (James 1:5)

Lord, you said all things were made through you and without you nothing was made that has been made. You also said the Son is the radiance of God's glory and the exact representation of your being, sustaining all things by his powerful word. You have said the Kingdom of God is righteousness, peace, and joy in the Holy Spirit. You also said the reason the Son of God appeared was to destroy the devil's work. So Lord, I declare the Internet and all social media were created by you and are owned by you. I declare they are transformed into platforms for the Kingdom of God. Have your way and take them over, destroying any content that is of the devil.
(John 1:3; Hebrews 1:3; Romans 14:17; 1 John 3:8)

Your word says "Do not envy the violent or choose any of their ways." Today Lord, I pray no one in this nation chooses to envy or repeat violence that is seen on television, in movies, in video games, or on the Internet. (Proverbs 3:31)

Your word says we are not to look with approval on anything vile. Lord, I ask you to reveal any vile content. Prevent those who are innocent without knowledge from accidental or intentional exposure to wicked content. I pray no one in America will look with approval or acceptance at anything that is wretched or vile. I speak an end to all wickedness and violence that is filling the eyes, minds, and hearts of young people in America today. (Psalm 101:3)

Father, your will is that we are sanctified and that we should avoid sexual immorality. You have said, "Among you, there must not be even a hint of sexual immorality, or any kind of impurity, or greed, because these are improper for God's holy people." I condemn and bind all sexually immoral content on television, on the Internet, in social media, and in any form of art or entertainment.
(1 Thessalonians 4:3; Ephesians 5:3)

Lord Jesus, you said, "You have heard that it was said, 'you shall not commit adultery.' But I tell you that anyone who looks at a woman lustfully has already committed adultery with her in his heart." I declare that all pornographic content is cursed and destroyed in the United States of America. I call an end to the pornography industry as men of God stop seeking and viewing pornography.
(Matthew 5:27-28; 1 Thessalonians 4:3)

Lord, as you spoke to the church through James, you said, "Therefore, get rid of all moral filth and the evil that is so prevalent and humbly accept the word planted in you, which can save you." I declare that every consumer of pornography immediately and intentionally repents and turns their heart and mind away from sexual immorality, thereby ridding themselves of all contact with filth and evil. (James 1:21)

Lord, there are many evils lurking in American society in the arts and entertainment. I ask you to expose and remove all wickedness and replace it with righteousness by both the creator and consumer. I receive, on behalf of America, all these covenant promises, by faith in your word, in the mighty and matchless name of Jesus Christ. Amen.

Your word says "Do not envy the violent
or choose any of their ways."

Today Lord, I pray no one in
this nation chooses to envy or repeat violence
that is seen on television, in movies,
in video games, or on the Internet.
(Proverbs 3:31)

SUGGESTIONS FOR EXPANDED PRAYERS FOR ARTS AND ENTERTAINMENT

Research and consider expanding your prayers for the following:

- Messages conveyed in movies, art displays and Internet-based art or entertainment

- Artists

- Actors, directors and producers of films

- Public art displays

- Local theater productions, including public and school-based

- Adult entertainment

Scan for free, step-by-step worksheets to prepare your expanded prayers.

Notes

PRAYER FOR ECONOMY

Finance and banking systems, credit, the economy, supply and demand, businesses, production, and manufacturing

Father, in the name of Jesus, I come to you for the economy of the United States of America. Lord, you said the love of money is the root of all evil. Therefore, I declare that the love of money is broken off every American. Your word says that your will is that all people prosper and have a bright hope and future. I pray all in America seek your truth and your will for their life. (Jeremiah 29:11)

You said everyone who meditates on your word day and night and delights in it is blessed. Your word says they will prosper in whatever they do. I declare that everyone in this nation will delight in the word of God and will prosper richly as they do so. (Psalm 1:1-3)

Lord, you said anyone who has been stealing must steal no longer but must work, doing something useful with their own hands, that they may have something to share with those in need. I pray for everyone in America who is now stealing, whether secretly, openly, fraudulently, or through carelessness, to be convicted by your Spirit to immediately stop. I pray they will repent of their wrong doing and seek proper employment. (Ephesians 4:28)

Lord, you have asked, "if someone wants to build a tower, won't they first sit down and count the cost before starting?" I pray every person in this nation will carefully evaluate and count the cost before making decisions and choices to expend money, whether it be an organizational, personal, or government decision.
(Luke 14:28)

Lord, you have said we are to owe no man anything except the debt of love. I pray that every person in America earnestly strives and takes appropriate action to pay off any current financial debt. I pray for those in financial debt to take full responsibility and accountability to repay the debt they incurred. (Romans 13:8) Lord, your word declares and you proved to Abraham that you are the Lord who will provide. I pray for those in debt to trust you as their provider. (Genesis 22:14)

Lord, you said we are to sow our seed in the morning and work in the evening because we do not know which of our works will succeed and prosper. I pray everyone in the United States of America invests in diverse instruments to ensure a harvest during any season. (Ecclesiastes 11:6)

Your word says all hard work brings a profit, but mere talk leads only to poverty. Father, I declare men desire to work hard and provide for themselves and their families. I declare the father of every child in America seeks gainful employment. (Proverbs 14:23)

I pray for your favor to rest on everyone in America. I ask you to establish their work and lead them to optimal success and joy, according to your word. (Psalm 90:17)

Lord, you have said you will bless our obedience to you and we will prosper. I declare that the wealth of America increases as you bless our obedience to you, and I declare a renewed seeking of obedience to your word. (Deuteronomy 28:4)

In Jesus' name, I declare and receive these benefits and blessings for America's obedience to you. In faith in you alone, I stand. Amen.

Your word says that
your will is that all people
prosper and have a bright hope
and future.

I pray all in America seek
your truth and your will
for their life.
(Jeremiah 29:11)

SUGGESTIONS FOR EXPANDED PRAYERS FOR ECONOMY

Research and consider expanding your prayers for the following:

- **Local businesses**

- **Charities and community support programs or organizations**

- **Employment and jobs**

- **Financial accountability**

- **Economic growth**

PRAYER FOR RELIGION

Heavenly Father, in the name of Jesus, I come to you for your church, created and built by your resurrected Son, Jesus Christ. I pray all believers make every effort to keep the unity of the Spirit through the bond of peace. (Ephesians 4:3)

Lord, you have warned believers to be aware of false teachers and prophets that infiltrate churches, seeking to preach and teach false gospels. I take authority over wicked, demonic, lying spirits in every church in America. Lord, reveal and expose them for the lies they speak.

I pray for the removal of every wrong spirit and person led by anything except a life surrendered and submitted to Jesus. Holy Spirit, reveal any wrong or lying spirits so ministers and pastors accurately discern and take appropriate action. (2 Corinthians 11:12-15)

When speaking of hypocritical leaders, Jesus, you said, "Every plant that my heavenly Father has not planted will be pulled up by the roots." Therefore, let any church leader not established by you be removed and replaced with one who wholeheartedly seeks and honors you. (Matthew 15:13)

I also declare that no believer is deceived by the wicked spirits of the antichrist and that there is absolute clarity for all people, as revealed by your Holy Spirit. (1 John 2:22)

I pray the eyes of everyone in America are open to see your salvation. I declare a great revival and movement of holiness breaks out and overtakes every community. (Luke 3:6)

Lord, you desire unity among us. I declare that all discord among believers ceases. I pray for believers to seek maturity in Christ through ever-increasing knowledge and wisdom of your word. (Psalm 133:1; Ephesians 4:4, 11-13)

Lord, I declare you have anointed your people to be strong in you and your mighty power. Let them boldly stand against and condemn evil. I pray every believer will seek continual victory for themselves and others as they use the full armor of God to defeat every wicked work. (Ephesians 6:10-17)

I pray for an increasing desire for prayer among your people as your Holy Spirit prompts their hearts. I declare believers will pray in the Spirit and with understanding on all occasions as we seek to bring your kingdom to all the earth. (1 Corinthians 14:15; Ephesians 6:18)

I declare Christians are strong and courageous to stand up and speak out against unrighteousness and ungodly leadership in every level of organization and government. Lord, bring a refreshed, holy boldness to the church to fully integrate into every sector of American society so that you and your truth prevail.
(Joshua 1:9; Acts 4:29, 31; Acts 14:13; Acts 28:31)

I declare believers are the light of the world. I pray the light of Jesus Christ in every believer will be visible through their good deeds.

I pray those who do not yet know you will see what believers have and say, "I want what you have!" (Matthew 5:14-16)

I declare the full Gospel of the Kingdom of God is preached in every city, rural town, and community in the United States of America and that the unsaved will turn to you and be saved. Lord, today, I declare that all in America come to the truth and choose to trust in Jesus alone.

I declare, as Jesus did, that no one comes to you, Father, except through Jesus Christ. (John 3:16; John 14:6)

In Jesus' name, I declare and receive all these things by faith in your word. I thank you, Father, that you are always faithful to perform your word. *Amen.*

SUGGESTIONS FOR EXPANDED PRAYERS FOR RELIGION

Research and consider expanding your prayers for the following:

- Local churches

- Unity among local churches

- Non-church ministries serving communities

- Expansion of the Gospel

Scan for free, step-by-step worksheets to prepare your expanded prayers.

Notes

By His Spirit; Through Our Prayer

CHANGE ONLY COMES BY THE SPIRIT OF GOD.

So he said to me, "This is the word of the Lord to Zerubbabel: 'Not by might nor by power, but by my Spirit,' says the Lord Almighty…" (Zechariah 4:6)

PRAYER STILL MOVES MOUNTAINS.

"Have faith in God," Jesus answered. "Truly I tell you, if anyone says to this mountain, 'Go, throw yourself into the sea,' and does not doubt in their heart but believes that what they say will happen, it will be done for them. Therefore I tell you, whatever you ask for in prayer, believe that you have received it, and it will be yours. And when you stand praying, if you hold anything against anyone, forgive them, so that your Father in heaven may forgive you your sins." (Mark 11:22-25)

WE CAN TRUST GOD HEARS AND ANSWERS.

I write these things to you who believe in the name of the Son of God so that you may know that you have eternal life. This is the confidence we have in approaching God: that if we ask anything according to his will, he hears us. And if we know that he hears us—whatever we ask—we know that we have what we asked of him. (1 John 5:13-15)

Prayer still moves Mountains.

Keys to Prayer

PRAY IN FAITH

Faith trusts and believes that what you cannot see will happen.

> *Without faith, it is impossible to please God, because if you come to Him, you must believe He exists and will reward you. (Hebrews 11:1, 6)*

PRAY THE WORD OF GOD

God has said that His word does not return to Him without effect. Rather, it accomplishes God's desire and purpose. Praying the word in faith is the key to activating God's power and re-aligning America with God. (Isaiah 55:11)

PRAY FOR GOD'S WILL AND KINGDOM TO COME TO EARTH

> *"This, then, is how you should pray: 'Our Father in heaven, hallowed be your name, your kingdom come, your will be done,'"(Matthew 6:9-10)*

Remember God's will is God's word. Praying His word brings His will.

PRAY AGAINST UNRIGHTEOUSNESS, NOT AGAINST PEOPLE

Our battle is not against people; it is against forces of spiritual wickedness causing people to do things that are against God and people. (Ephesians 6:12)

PRAY IN THE NAME OF JESUS

Jesus told His disciples to ask the Father in His name, and they will receive. (John 16:23-26; 1 John 5:14-15)

References

Cunningham, Loren. *The Seven Spheres of Influence*. YWAM Podcast.
YWAM Network, 2016.
(https://ywampodcast.net/shows/teaching/the-seven-spheres-of-
influence-loren-cunningham)

Enlow, Johnny. *The Seven Mountain Prophecy: Unveiling the Coming Elijah
Revolution*. Lake Mary, FL: Creation House, 2008.

O'Brien, Bronwyn. *The 7 Mountains of Influence-A Practical Guide for
Understanding God's Purpose for Your Life*. Victoria, Australia: Global
Publishing Group, 2011. Digital edition: Amazon.com and
(https://www.the7mountains.com)

Wallnau, Lance. *Invading Babylon: the 7 Mountain Mandate*.
Shippensburg, PA: Destiny Image, 2013.

ABOUT THE AUTHOR

Ruth Ann Nylen, PHD is the author of *The Radical Power of God* and founded Really Good News Ministries in 2007.

She earned a BA and MA in Christian Theology from Life Christian University and a PHD in Curriculum and Instruction from The University of Kansas.

She feeds her passion to inspire, equip and encourage believers to personal growth and purpose in Christ through writing and developing resources and practical tools. Visit her at ruthannnylen.com

Scan for more resources and to connect with the author.

www.ingramcontent.com/pod-product-compliance
Lightning Source LLC
Chambersburg PA
CBHW071633040426
42452CB00009B/1599